CW00686745

This book is to be returned on or before the date above.
It may be borrowed for a further period if not in demand.

Essex County Council
Libraries

No Picnic

A Play

George MacEwan Green

Samuel French – London
New York – Sydney – Toronto – Hollywood

CHARACTERS

Fiona Parmiter ⎫
Frank Chaseforth ⎪ young English students on holiday
Dennis Threswaite ⎬
Poppy Gorsham ⎭
Esther Jakobson, a young German Jewess
Karl Ernstetter, a young German in the Hitler Youth
  Movement
Voice of a narrator

The action of the play takes place in a rural part of
Germany on a summer's day

Time—1938

COSTUMES

Frank is dressed in blazer, flannels, and Panama hat. His shirt-neck is open and he wears a silk cravat.

Dennis is rather similarly dressed, except that he is minus the cravat and instead of a Panama he has a jaunty Tyrolean hat set far back on his head.

Fiona, **Poppy**, and **Esther** wear summery dresses of the period, but, where indicated in the closing sequence of the play, **Esther** wears the pyjama-striped dress of a concentration camp inmate.

Karl wears a brown shirt, dark shorts, and almost-knee length white socks. He has a swastika arm-band on his right arm and wears a Sam Browne type belt with a leather-holstered revolver at his side.

NO PICNIC*

A hillside. Germany. Summer 1938

A bare stage. The background indicates a blue sky above a place of greenery

When the play opens the stage is deserted, but voices, initially faint, growing louder, are heard, both laughing and complaining

Poppy (*off*) I'm dying, I'm dying. I've never climbed so high before. (*With a screaming laugh*) Oooh! I'm slipping. Someone help me.

The sound of male laughter is heard off

You rotten things, help me. Dennis!

Dennis (*off, laughing*) I can't right now, Poppy, I think I'm about to black-out from lack of oxygen.

Poppy (*off*) Such chivalry! Frank, you help me.

Fiona (*off*) Don't you dare let go of my hand, Frank Chaseforth.

Frank (*off*) Dear oh dear, is this the spirit that made the Empire great? Precious few bounds will you lot set wider still and wider. Come on now, this isn't Everest, it's only——(*Startled*) Oooh-oops! . . .

Dennis (*off, laughing*) You were saying, Frank?

Frank (*off*) . . . a molehill, my dear Dennis. (*Triumphantly*) A piddling little molehill which Fiona and I have now sur-mounted.

Frank now enters R, *leading Fiona after him by the hand*

Frank takes bounding, exhuberant steps, but Fiona appears limp and breathless. Frank carries a picnic basket. He releases Fiona's hand and lays the picnic basket down. He goes C. *He strikes a legs-astride pose and flamboyantly removes his cravat which he then waves jubilantly*

---

*N.B. Paragraph 3 on page ii of this Acting Edition regarding photocopying and video-recording should be carefully read.

I hereby claim sovereignty of this molehill in the name of His Britannic Majesty King George the vee-eye.

Fiona sinks exhaustedly to the ground

Fiona (*breathlessly*) When—when you're quite—oh, dear—finished with your histrionics, I suggest you give a hand to Dennis and Poppy. (*Looking off* R) They both seem to have gone into reverse gear.

Frank (*in mock Blimpish voice*) How spittingly shame-making for dear old England. (*He strides* R, *bellowing loudly*) Come along, you lazy landlubbers, put some oomph into it.

Dennis (*off*) Shut-up, you chauvinistic swine, and do something constructive.

Frank This, Dennis Threswaite, you intellectual weed, is where I'll show you how invaluable is my boy-scout ever-preparedness.

Frank exits R. *Almost immediately he reappears. He holds one end of his cravat, whilst Dennis, who follows, holds the other end. With his other hand Dennis grips Poppy's hand, as she totters behind him*

Poppy carries a portable gramophone. All three flop down on to the stage beside Fiona

Dennis I do believe that for the past fortnight we've been stuffing ourselves with too many German sausages and too many German beers for our own good.

Frank Speak for yourself, weed. I negotiated the hill with comparative ease.

Dennis Yes, Frank, yes, we know you're most frightfully athletic. Quite the little Douglas Fairbanks, aren't we?

Frank (*playfully punching Dennis*) Bitchy. (*He gets to his feet and strikes an exaggerated boxing pose*) Come along then, Threswaite, show your mettle in a few rounds of fisticuffs—if you dare.

Fiona Such infants, are they not, Poppy?

Poppy Overgrown schoolboys, Fiona.

Dennis gets up

Dennis (*to Fiona*) Tush, Miss Parmiter. (*To Poppy*) Tut, Miss Gorsham. Do you not comprehend that gentlemen must address themselves to questions of honour in time-proven manner?

Fiona Honour, he says. Where was honour when poor Poppy here had to lug that gramophone up the hill?

Dennis Unfair, Fiona, unfair. Isn't that unfair, Frank?

Frank Absolutely.

Fiona Why is it unfair, Frank?

Frank Naturally, because . . . Why *is* it unfair, Dennis?

Dennis Because I offered to carry it. You heard me offer, didn't you, Frank? Immediately we left the hotel. Well, almost immediately. And Poppy would have none of it, would she, Frank?

Frank Absolutely. Now, do let's have our fight. It'll be time to have the picnic soon.

Dennis I must settle this gramophone business first. I mean to say, unmentionable things are being hinted at.

Frank Really? What unmentionable things?

Dennis ⎫ (*together*) ⎰ I would rather not mention them.
Frank ⎭   ⎱ You would rather not mention them.

Poppy I refused your half-hearted offer because the damn thing belongs to my Great-Aunt Ethel—I only borrowed it for the holiday—and if I should let either of you get your hands on it, I know it would end up in a thousand bits within five minutes.

Frank Do you concur with that slanderous sentiment, Dennis?

Dennis Indubitably.

Frank Yes, so do I. Now may we indulge in fisticuffs?

Dennis But, of course.

Poppy (*to Fiona*) I can't afford to upset Great-Aunt Ethel, because I'm fairly positive I'm in her last Will and whatsit. She's vulgarly rich, you know.

Frank and Dennis move downstage and adopt ridiculous poses, as if ready to commence battle

Fiona If one has to be vulgar, rich vulgar is best.

Poppy Everyone thought she was dying back in twenty-eight, but she took up South American dancing and now, ten years later, at the age of seventy-eight she's as fit as a fiddle.

Dennis Usual rules, what?

Frank Indeed. The first one to dislodge an eye from its socket will be declared the winner, especially if it's his opponent's eye.

Dennis And any contestant choking to death on his own blood will be deemed to have conceded victory to the opposition.

Frank Right.

Dennis Right.

Frank and Dennis begin to skip around on toe-point, feinting, never once coming within a mile of hitting one another. They breathe heavily and grunt, as if they are in most deadly earnest

Frank Give in?
Dennis Not on your life.
Fiona I wonder they don't tire of these silly games.
Poppy I don't see the point of it.
Fiona Evidently the point of it is that there is no point to it. It's their own version of what they once saw at some music-hall.
Poppy Good grief, imagine anyone paying good money to see that puerile stuff.

Frank and Dennis are still "boxing" without ever coming to blows

Frank (*gasping*) The mist—the damnable red mist—it's clouding my eyes.
Dennis (*also gasping*) Me—too. But my—my mist isn't just red— no, no—it's—it's scarlet.
Frank So is mine—now. Scarlet—like—like blood.
Dennis And mine—mine is scarlet—like—like gore.
Frank (*standing still, hands on waist, no longer gasping, and using acid voice*) And mine, you cheeky baggage, is scarlet like bloody gore.
Dennis (*adopting similar pose and voice*) But mine is scarleter and bloodier and gorier. So there, dearie.
Frank When my red mist comes I am a demon possessed.
Dennis And I'm turned into a raging bull.
Frank Raging bull? Silly cow, more like.
Dennis Demon possessed? Dispossessed fairy, I'd say.
Frank Ooh, you, I should slap your wrists.
Dennis You and what army?
Frank You've gone too far.

Frank makes a sudden movement and knocks the hat from Dennis's head

Dennis Foul, foul, foul. (*Turning to girls*) I appeal to you, ladies.
Fiona Thank goodness, this is nearly the end of the routine.
Frank Appeal to the ladies? You wouldn't appeal to a sex-starved telegraph pole.

Dennis I do not wish to know that.

Fiona whispers into Poppy's ear

Frank (*observing Fiona and Poppy*) I think, old bean, the audience grows restless.

Dennis Bother the audience. (*Pauses*) I know, let's skip the rest and go straight to the punchline.

Frank Splendid idea. You first.

Dennis Then it's through thick and thin, my friend?

Dennis and Frank shake hands

Frank Through fire and flood, old pal.

Dennis Through fair and foul, dear comrade.

Frank Through storm and tempest.

Dennis Until we meet again.

Frank Tomorrow.

Dennis Providing it isn't raining.

Frank Or as long as it isn't too hot.

Poppy (*rising*) I say, Dennis, how about taking a bit of a stroll with me? I'd like to look for some Alpine plants to take home to Great-Aunt Ethel.

Dennis (*releasing Frank's hand. Surprised*) What? (*Eagerly*) Yes, rather. Oh, yes, that would be spiffing.

Poppy (*beginning to exit* L) Come on then.

Dennis (*stooping to retrieve his hat*) Coming, Poppy, coming.

Dennis quickly joins Poppy. They exit L

Frank (*amazed*) What was that all about?

Fiona I expect Poppy was just bored. Your little games are an acquired taste.

Frank I don't know why Poppy came on this holiday. She's been very brusque with poor Dennis up until now. She's hardly given him the time of day, far less any hint at the time of night.

Fiona Everyone can't be expected to see Dennis through your eyes, you know.

Frank If you ask me, she doesn't like men at all very much.

Fiona Quite possibly. Poppy's very intelligent in her own way.

Frank Hey, had you something to do with sending them off on their own? I saw you whisper to Poppy. (*Admiringly*) Why you sly, lovely, gorgeous little minx, you're up to some little ploy, aren't you?

Frank goes to kneel beside Fiona. He puts an arm around her

Frank Wouldn't it be rather wonderful if Poppy and Dennis did hit it off?

Fiona Wonderful for them?

Frank And for us. Last night of the holiday and all that. We could perhaps—well, you know ...

Fiona What?

Frank Switch rooms.

Fiona I'm not sure I understand.

Frank Share differently. Instead of me sharing with Dennis, we could ...

Fiona Oh, I see. I doubt if Poppy's quest for Alpine plants will stretch as far as that. She's a pretty moral sort of girl.

Frank Damn her. (*Drawing even closer to Fiona, his embrace becoming more emphatic*) You know, darling, this past fortnight has been pure torture, being so near to you, wanting you so desperately, yet never being properly alone.

Frank attempts to kiss Fiona, but she gently repels him

Frank What is it?

Fiona (*rising*) Not just now, Frank.

Fiona walks downstage L where she stands, arms folded, her back towards Frank

Fiona Frank, I have to tell you something.

Frank Well?

Fiona I'm pregnant.

Frank What did you say?

Fiona Pregnant, Frank, pregnant.

Frank (*leaping to his feet*) You mean you're going to have a baby?

Fiona No, Frank. I said I am pregnant. I did *not* say I was going to have a baby.

Frank (*obviously puzzled*) But if you're ... (*Pauses. Enlightened. Speaking roughly*) I see, you mean you're going to get rid of it—is that it?

Fiona Abort it, Frank.

Frank Are you sure?

Fiona About abortion?

Frank No, about being pregnant.

Fiona Yes, about that I am quite sure. I had tests.

Frank When for God's sake?

Fiona Before we left Oxford.

Frank You knew before we came on this holiday?

Fiona Yes.

Frank And never said a word?

Fiona No.

Frank But why?

Fiona Because—Oh, I don't know. Because I didn't want to spoil the holiday, I suppose.

Frank I wonder what you think you're doing now.

Fiona Also, I think, because I hadn't quite worked things out in my own mind.

Frank I see. And now you've got it all cut and dried, is that it?

Fiona Yes. (*Pauses*) No. (*Pauses*) I just had to think about it by myself.

Frank And why choose this precise moment to impart the glad tidings?

Fiona Don't be pompous, Frank. I'm telling you now, because now is when I've decided to tell you. I'm not trying to spoil anything, or upset you, or be a nuisance, or anything like that. But, well, this *is* the last day of the holiday. Tomorrow we go home and then . . .

Frank I *am* the father, aren't I?

Fiona turns angrily towards him, but then speaks only with sad accusation

Fiona Oh, Frank!

Frank Well, there was that picture of you in the *Tatler* with young Lord Whatshisname at the hunt ball. If you ask me, that was a pretty amorous clinch he had you in when the pair of you were lolling, champagne glass in hand, on the steps of that noble stairway.

Fiona (*without rancour*) Don't be petty, Frank. I told you at the time it was a drunken grope and that I slapped his face as soon as the photographer moved on.

Frank places his hands over his face

Frank (*muffled voice*) I'm sorry.

Fiona What?

Frank (*removing hands from face*) I'm sorry, I'm sorry, I'm sorry.
(*Laughing wryly*) God, you know how to floor a chap, Fiona.
I'm glad you waited with this news until after we had climbed
this blasted hill; the way my legs are trembling I'd never have
made it otherwise. (*Laughing again*) We only—I mean, just the
once or twice—and this happens.

Fiona Yes, it's hard lines.

Frank Talk about the luck of the Chaseforths. Rumour always
has it that one in every ten thousand of those things are made of
faulty rubber. Trust me to hit the ten thousand mark. They say
it's done deliberately as a sop to the Church, or the League of
Purity, or some bunch of holy rollers. Bloody rotters.

Fiona Whatever, it's done, and now we must be sensible about it.

Frank It? Yes, I suppose it is an "it" at this stage; not him; not her;
just poor bloody it.

Fiona Don't be maudlin. Frank. Sentimentality isn't your forte—
you can't sustain it, for you don't believe it. So let's try to
address ourselves to practicalities.

Frank I think I might be entitled to shed a tear or two for the child
I'll never know.

Fiona (*angrily*) You can be a right bloody brute when you want
to, Frank Chaseforth. I'm going to be the one who'll have to go
through the whole disgusting performance, so instead of adopting that accusing attitude—and that's exactly what you're
doing—you should damn well be turning your mind to thinking
about ways of giving me support.

Frank Support? Money, you mean?

Fiona Yes, money. I can come up with some myself, but I'm going
to need more. I could get it done on the cheap in some back alley
place . . .

Frank (*alarmed*) Christ, no, Fiona, don't do that.

Fiona . . . but I've no intention of doing that. There's a Harley Street
man who handles such matters, only he's damned expensive.
Safe and clean and discreet, but terribly, terribly expensive.

Frank I can well believe it. But you're right, as always. If it has to
be done, it should be done by the best.

Fiona So, can you help? With money, I mean.

Frank You know my people keep me on a pretty tight rein when it comes to the old shekels, but I'll dig it up somehow. Any idea how much?

Fiona Somewhere around the two hundred guineas mark, I think.

Frank Holy Moses!

Fiona I know, it's a lot. On the other hand, he runs a rare old risk. His career's in ruins if he's found out, not to mention the prospect of several years behind bars.

Frank And it's a seller's market, I suppose.

Fiona I could come up with almost half without involving my people.

Frank I'll raise the balance some way.

Fiona I don't want you to get sucked in by money-lenders, or to have a millstone hung round your neck by some bunch of Jews.

Frank comes downstage to Fiona. He takes her hand

Frank It's all right, my darling, I'm really not such a fool as I make out I am. (*Drawing her to him in an embrace*) God, it's queer, isn't it? Here we are, two bright young things, the products of wealth and breeding, with the benefit of university education, but when something like this happens we're about as ineffectual as any common labourer and his shopgirl. The labourer and his shopgirl would probably get married, have their brat, and keep their consciences clean.

Fiona Don't even think like that, Frank. It can't be like that for us.

Frank No, it's not for us. We're intelligent. Besides, we know a man in Harley Street, don't we?

Fiona Yes, and some way we'll afford him, for we both know, Frank, that we can't afford to ruin our lives with a marriage of that kind.

Frank But I *do* love you.

Fiona And I you. But I'm not sure I love you enough to marry you and then calmly accept that all I want to do with my life must be sacrificed. It would be a disaster for both of us.

Frank Life is cruel, what?

Fiona Beastly, darling, beastly.

Frank But we'll lick it somehow.

Fiona Because we must.

Frank Does anyone else know?

Fiona No, it's our secret.

Frank Not even Poppy?

Fiona God, least of all Poppy. And you mustn't tell Dennis.

Frank As if I would.

Fiona Well, you might blurt it out when you've had a drink too many and when you either wax self-pitying or boastful.

Frank Sometimes I think you must have an awfully low opinion of me, my dear.

Fiona No, I don't. I just see you as you are and accept it and love you for it—most of the time.

Frank I'll settle for that any day of the week—it's probably a lot more than I deserve.

Frank and Fiona kiss. There is the sound of angry voices from off left. Fiona looks anxiously towards the voices

Fiona Look out, they're coming back. Don't let them see anything's amiss.

Frank Don't worry. I promise to be my usual scintillatingly silly self.

Frank and Fiona draw apart

Poppy, striding angrily, enters L, *closely followed by Dennis whose arms are outspread, as if declaring innocence*

Dennis But what did I do that was so awful, Poppy?

Frank (*to Poppy*) Didn't you get your plants, sweetie?

Poppy No sweetie, I didn't get my plants. A fat chance I had of getting plants when your friend there was behaving like—like . . .

Frank Ooh, do tell all.

Poppy Like a whirling dervish, that's what like.

Fiona Whatever's wrong, Poppy?

Poppy (*whirling round to point at Dennis*) That—that's what's wrong.

Frank looks questioningly at Dennis. Dennis shrugs

Fiona Dennis, what did you do?

Dennis Nothing. Absolutely nothing.

The others continue to look sceptical

That is, I mean to say, almost nothing. Hardly anything.

Poppy Liar! For a kick-off you breathed.

Frank (*feigning outrage*) Good grief, laddie, have you been breathing again? Haven't I warned you about that time out of number?

Dennis I can't help it. I'm so afraid I'll die if I stop.

Frank But you'll go blind if you insist on doing it.

Poppy Very hilarious. He wasn't just breathing, he was breathing down my neck.

Frank Heaven preserve us, Dennis, have you no shame? Breathing down Poppy's neck. Is that your current perversion, boy?

Dennis It just happened to be the way my mouth was pointing.

Frank I blame all those American films. They're bound to affect immature minds.

Poppy And then he touched me.

Frank T-touched you? Where? I demand to know where.

Poppy I would rather not say.

Frank Dennis? Come on, laddie, spit it out. Where did you touch Poppy? You'll feel better if you make a clean breast of it.

Dennis I touched her on the upper slopes.

Fiona Stop it, you two. Poppy has every right to be upset. Dennis, you behaved like a cad.

Dennis No, I didn't. I wanted to, but she wouldn't let me.

Poppy Of course I wouldn't let you. Do you think I'm the sort of girl who welcomes improper advances?

Frank (*in mock sadness*) Dennis, Dennis, Dennis. Improper advances. Is there no end to this catalogue of disgusting behaviour? Is there no limit to your lustful appetite?

Dennis I hope I am no more than a normal red-blooded Englishman, and when a young lady invites me to go gathering Alpine plants for her Great-Aunt Ethel I trust I possess enough *savoir-faire* to read between the lines and know which way the wind is blowing.

Poppy Mixed metaphors excuse nothing.

Fiona Quite right, Poppy dear. We'll ignore these louts and make a start on the picnic. (*Quietly*) Was Dennis really foul?

Poppy (*also quietly*) Of course not. As a matter of fact it was rather nice, only I don't intend that he should know that.

Fiona puts an arm around Poppy's waist and guides her upstage to the picnic hamper. There they both kneel, and from the picnic hamper bring out a chequered cloth, cutlery, crockery, glasses etc.

Frank (*ham-acting*) It looks to me, old chap, as if you have possibly fallen foul of the damsels.

Dennis sullenly kicks the ground with his toe and responds with his own "ham"

Dennis Women! If there's a way of doing a chap down you can bet your bottom dollar they'll find it.

Frank Not for nothing are they dubbed *les belles dames sans merci*. Never mind, bosom pal, you've still got me. And my advice to you is that you must go straight back in at the deep end. So off you go and ask Poppy if you may play her Great-Aunt's gramophone to while away the time.

Dennis (*horrified*) I wouldn't ask her permission now to play with anything belonging to her. She'd probably start shouting "rape" at the top of her voice, bringing every German shepherd within a ten miles radius running to her aid.

Frank Dennis, Dennis, you mustn't let one little misunderstanding throw you so completely. You must be firm. You must be ruthless. You must be masterful. Women love that and, after all, Poppy is merely another woman.

Dennis I wish I could be sure about that.

Poppy The children are playing their games again.

Fiona So one hears.

Frank Go on, Dennis, ask her—no, tell her we intend to make use of her instrument.

Dennis And if she refuses to co-operate?

Frank Look menacing and brooding and smouldering and all that sort of thing, don't you know?

Dennis (*making a grotesque face*) Like this?

Frank (*feigning fright, backing away*) Yes, something like that, only a shade less Count Dracula and a bit more Valentino.

Dennis (*making an even worse face*) Is this better?

Frank I meant Valentino when he was still alive. Never mind, it'll do. Now off you go.

Dennis goes to Poppy and Fiona

Dennis (*in small voice*) Poppy, may we please utilize your dear Great-Aunt Ethel's phonographic machine?

Poppy (*looking up*) What? What did you say?
Dennis Oh, nothing.

Dennis turns towards downstage again, but stops upon a signal from Frank

Frank Her master's voice, Dennis, her master's voice.
Dennis You mean I should bark?
Poppy Oh, stop your nonsense, the pair of you. I'll put a record on for you, but I won't have you messing around with my things.
Dennis Thank you very much, Poppy. That's really very sweet of you.

Dennis returns downstage to join Frank and they watch whilst Poppy opens up the gramophone, winds it, puts on a record and plays it. It is a nineteen-thirties tune of the thé dansant *variety*

(*To Frank*) You were one hundred per cent right, old man: the masterful approach worked beautifully. She's practically eating out of my hand now. (*After a pause*) Well, at least she didn't bite my leg.
Frank Stout fellow, you bowled her over completely. You've tamed her savage breast.
Dennis A bit more time and I could have tamed her other breast as well.
Frank Now, whilst the iron is hot, let's invite them to cut a rug with us. (*In a raised voice*) Ladies, how do you fancy a spot of the old light fantastic?
Fiona What a splendid idea. What do you say, Poppy?
Poppy Jolly good.

Fiona and Poppy rise and begin to dance with one another

Frank Dennis, I do believe our own petards have just been hoisted on.
Dennis But are we dismayed?
Frank Yes.
Dennis Yes, we are. But we mustn't show it.
Frank Shall we?
Dennis Shall we not?
Frank We shall, but bags I lead.

Frank and Dennis now dance with one another

Frank Wretched floor, what?

Dennis Mmm. You'd think they'd weed it once in a while.

Fiona Your reverse chassé is quite beautiful.

Frank Thank you.

Fiona I was speaking to Poppy.

Esther, panting, dishevelled, dashes on from R. She collides with the dancing couples and emits a sound of mixed panic and frustration

Frank I say, Fraulein, this isn't an excuse-me.

Esther Please, please, let me go.

Esther attempts to brush past, but Frank impedes her progress

Frank No use dashing, Miss, the last bus went ages ago. You've no hope of catching it now and there won't be another for years.

Esther Let me go! They're after me. Don't you understand, they're after me.

Dennis I know, it's a paper chase.

Frank If it is, then she's run clean out of paper.

Fiona Don't. Can't you see, she's really terrified? Poppy, put that damn gramophone off. (*To Esther*) What's wrong? Who's after you?

Poppy goes and stops the gramophone

Esther Please, just let me go. They're right behind me.

Frank Who?

Esther Nazis. Now, please, let me go.

Frank Hey, calm down, Fraulein. It can't be as bad as all that.

Esther You don't understand.

Fiona But where are you running to?

Esther What? (*She looks about her. She is sobbing and shouting*) I don't know, I don't know. (*Between sobs*) They came for us all, all the Jews in the town. We saw them coming to our house. Through the window we saw them coming. Pappa said, "So this is it," and Mamma said, "God help us all". Then Pappa said, "Run, Esther, run. Go out the back way. Run to the hills." I went. I was so afraid. As I went out the back door I could hear them hammering on the front door. Pappa was saying, "All right, all right, hold your horses". He was going to the door, but slowly, so that I could get a good start. I heard Mamma weeping. But still I ran. God forgive me, I left my Pappa and Mamma and ran for my life. I ran for the hills, but then I heard someone shout, "There's the daughter. There's Esther Jakobson getting away. After her before she escapes." But you don't understand, do you? You are nice civilized people and so you can't even begin to understand.

Fiona (*putting her arms around Esther*) We'll try to understand, but you must calm yourself.

Poppy Yes, whatever it is, we'll help you to get it sorted out. You see, we are English! English, do you understand?

Esther No, no, I must just run. I must escape. Oh, can't you see, can't you see?

Frank I'm sure she's not a criminal or anything. Something has happened to put her into this state, but probably she's got hold of a stick by the wrong end.

Dennis Mind you, they're pretty rum about Jews, these Nazis.

Poppy But surely they wouldn't terrorize a young girl into such a state as this.

Esther laughs and sobs hysterically

Esther You are so blind, you foreigners. They cage us up like animals, they torture us, they kill us, but you don't see because you are blind. They—they—they do awful things, terrible things, by the light of day, under the sun, without shame, without fear, because they know you are all blind and will see nothing, say nothing, do nothing.

Frank We won't let anything happen to you. I promise that.

Esther Just let me go. You can't do anything else for me. Just let me run and run and run.

Karl enters running R. He stops abruptly

Esther turns, sees Karl, and screams

Karl (*slightly breathless*) So, there you are, Esther. You've acted very foolishly in giving the authorities so much trouble. Now, come back down to the town with me and let us leave these foreign guests to have their picnic. (*To the others*) I am right in assuming you are going to have a picnic, yes? It is a perfect day for such recreation. I am only sorry our little Esther has interrupted your pleasantries.

Esther (*clinging to Fiona*) Don't let him take me. Please, please, you mustn't let him take me.

Karl Come along, Esther, there has been enough upset for one day. This isn't like you to behave in such an irresponsible manner.

Frank This young lady seems to think you want to take her to prison. If that is so, may we enquire the nature of her crime?

Karl As aliens in Germany, albeit very welcome aliens, this matter does not concern you in the least.

Dennis Rot, old boy. Why, it's our bounden duty to help any lady in distress. Ain't that so, Frank?

Frank Of course, it is.

Poppy Besides, we aren't aliens. We're all English.

Fiona And you must admit, it's rather unusual in a civilized land for a young female to be hunted across the countryside, unless she's a criminal of some kind, or unless some criminal act is being perpetrated against her.

Karl I repeat, this is a purely German matter. (*Pauses. He smiles*) Nevertheless, I do see your point of view. Believe me, if ever I found myself in a similar situation in your country, my reactions would probably be exactly the same as yours. (*To Esther*) Oh, Esther, do you not see the trouble your foolishness is causing? (*To the others*) I do not know what far-fetched stories Fraulein Jakobson has been spinning to you, but I can assure you that there is no great mystery and certainly no harm is intended to anyone. Why, Esther and I know one another very well.

Frank Is this true, Esther? Do you know this chap?

Esther Know him? I thought once I did, yes. We were childhood friends and High School students together, Karl Ernstetter and I.

Karl There, I said so, didn't I?

Esther But now he wears that uniform of the Hitler Youth and goes strutting around giving everyone orders. Even some of his own people laughed at his new-found pomposity—at first.

Karl You are being stupidly spiteful, Esther.

Esther Do you know, in the kindergarten Karl and I used to share the same desk. We used to play together. He was such a nice boy. My parents and his parents were good friends. But now— now Karl wears his uniform and his swastika armband and helps the Gestapo to round up the Jews for the concentration camps.

Karl Concentration camps! That is wild, malicious talk. It is such talk that reveals the true nature of the Jewish conspiracy. It is designed to bring the Fatherland into disrepute in the eyes of the world.

Frank All right, if not to a concentration camp, where *do* you want to take Esther?

Karl To be with her people. To be with her own kind. To be with her father and mother. Is that such a dreadful thing?

Fiona But where?

Karl I do not pretend to know the exact geographical location. Probably somewhere in the east. Under an edict of our democratically-elected Fuehrer these people—the Jews, I mean—are to be re-settled in one particular part of Germany. There they can follow their own religion, their own way of life. They will still be a part of the state, but separate. Scattered about our country, as they are, they cause nothing but mischief, always seeking to erode the fabric of the nation, delighting in contaminating the Aryan blood, draining us of our wealth, our culture, our spiritual strength. The Führer could, if he wished, throw every last one of them out of our country, or even destroy their entire race, but he is a humane man. He seeks only to rehabilitate them in mass; to isolate them so that the infection they breed will not bring ruin and death to the rest of the nation.

Dennis Sounds a bit drastic, I must say.

Karl A drastic cure for a drastic disease, good Sir. But it *is* a cure. And it will eventually be seen by all reasonable people to be a kind one. Yes, even Esther here may one day be forced to admit that it is the best and wisest solution. My God, don't you see how we act in broad daylight? If we were hell-bent on destroying people like Esther would we not do it under cover of darkness and in secret?

Poppy (*to the others*) He does have a point there, you've got to admit.

Karl Of course, I do, Miss. Why, if we were really intending to do them some dreadful harm, wouldn't it be more easily accomplished by separating them from one another? Wouldn't that weaken them more quickly? But no, we keep their families intact. We compensate them for any property they have to leave

behind. Some people might even say that we are being dangerously weak in making so many concessions. But we are Germans and we are by nature fair and open and honest in our
dealings with others, even those who have always boasted of
being different from us, intellectually superior to us, and who
have made it a way of life to extract every last penny from us.

Frank Esther?

Esther The kindest thing I can think is that Karl believes the lies
he tells. I hope that is so, for the sake of the good times when we
were children. For his conscience's sake, I pray he deceives only
because he, himself, is deceived. Yes, we shall be re-settled, but it
will be behind barbed wire and, eventually, under the earth
itself.

Karl That is the scare-mongering talk of the Jews. It is the evil
elders of your own race, Esther Jakobson, steeped bone-deep in
their long accumulation of sins, who tell such tales to their
young people in order to make them defiant and unruly and a
danger to the Aryan people.

Frank It seems to me that you are both convinced of your separate
truths. It is very hard, I must say, for outsiders to judge
objectively between you.

Karl And you have no right to judge. It is sufficient for you to
recognize that at this moment I represent the properly estab-
lished authority of Germany, in which country you and your
friends are merely guests.

Frank All the same, upon humanitarian grounds—and since even
you don't claim that the fraulein is an actual criminal—I suggest
that you let her remain with us in order to give her time to make
up her own mind as to whether or not she wishes to participate
in this re-settlement scheme. No-one should be required to make
such a big choice under bullying pressure.

Dennis Damn right.

Karl That is quite out of the question. The choice has already been
made for her.

Fiona Not by her parents.

Karl It has been made by the German people. I have been very
patient, but all discussion is now ended. Esther Jakobson, the
Jewess, will come back down to the town in my custody and that
will be that.

Frank Like hell it will.

Karl You will not be so foolish as to try to stop me from performing my duty.

Dennis And why not?

Karl withdraws his revolver from its holster and points it

Karl Because I will use this if I am forced to.

Poppy My God, is that thing loaded?

Frank Loaded or not, it's pure bluff. Herr Ernstetter, you wouldn't dare shoot any innocent holiday-makers.

Dennis Your tourist trade would end up as flat as an old punctured tyre.

Karl We in Germany are no longer controlled by money-grabbing Jews, as you in England still are. Our national honour is now more important to us than grovelling for money from mindless foreigners.

Fiona (*relaxing her embrace of Esther*) I don't believe anything he says, but I think we'd be daft to goad him into using that thing.

Poppy Fiona's right, Frank. We must see sense.

Frank Good grief, if he used that pop-gun he'd be creating the kind of incident that starts wars, and he damn well knows it. That wouldn't please Herr Hitler one little bit at a time when he's negotiating peace with Mr Neville Chamberlain.

Karl I think I know better than you what would please the Führer. (*Laughing*) And it seems to us that your Mr Chamberlain doesn't have a gun either.

Poppy Frank, you've no right to endanger us all just because you feel bloody-minded.

Frank What do you say, Dennis?

Dennis We've tried our best, but, as the girls say, it's no use arguing with a gun. (*He pauses*) But I do think this chap should give us his word of honour that what he has said about this re-settlement business is true.

Esther No! I, too, am a German and I, too, have a care for Germany's honour, so I will relieve Karl from the necessity of betraying his honour and that of our country with any more lies by agreeing to go quietly with him. It is true: the unarmed cannot argue reason with an opponent who has a revolver pointed at their heads. Besides, where would I run to? There are no safe places left in Germany. So concentration camp, or idyllic re-settlement, I would rather be with Pappa and Mamma and among my own brave people.

Karl All this unpleasantness could have been avoided if you had behaved reasonably in the first place, Esther. But reasonable behaviour, alas, cannot be expected from Jews.

Frank (*to Esther*) Are you sure about this decision?

Esther (*wiping her tears*) Oh, I am very sure. Escape was just a stupid fancy, a silly Jewish day-dream, an immature female weakness.

Esther moves from the others and stands by Karl

Esther I am ready.

Frank At least put that bloody gun away.

Karl Not quite yet. I'll not put it away until I'm sure there will be not attempt at tiresome English heroics. My apologies for disturbing your picnic. Please carry on now. (*He raises his arm in salute*) Heil Hitler.

Dennis (*raising his arm*) *Heil* good old Neville.

Karl (*to Esther*) Walk in front.

Esther and Karl exit R *watched dismally by the others*

Frank (*emotions exploding*) Christ, if only I'd had a gun!

Fiona Gently, Frank, gently. It's done now. It's over. There was nothing else we could do.

Dennis What an arrogant swine he was.

Poppy If you ask me, both were typical Germans: he playing the conquering hero, she playing the plucky little victim.

Fiona (*quietly*) Shut up, Poppy dear.

Frank Yes, sweetie, shut up.

Poppy But I'm only saying that together they were playing out some stupid German game—a bit like those stupid games that you and Dennis are so fond of—and outsiders just don't understand them and shouldn't interfere in them.

Frank We can't consider ourselves outsiders any longer, though.

There is a great roll of thunder

Fiona (*startled*) What's that?

Frank Thunder rolling over the hills.

Fiona Heavens, for a moment I thought it was the sound of guns.

Another roll of thunder

Dennis (*looking up*) Looks ominous, what?

Frank Yes, I think our little hill-top is going to come under the clouds at any moment.

More thunder

Fiona I think we've had it as far as the picnic is concerned. Best pack up before the rain comes.

Poppy Dear God, Great-Aunt Ethel's gramophone. If that gets ruined in a rain storm I can kiss my legacy good-bye.

Fiona (*to Frank and Dennis*) Come on, you two, give me a hand to pack up.

Poppy goes to the gramophone, takes off the record, and closes up the gramophone. Fiona, Frank, and Dennis gather up all the picnic things and stow them away in the hamper. They stand in a group L, Poppy holding the gramophone, Frank holding the picnic hamper

Karl enters R. He stands facing the audience

There is the sound of more thunder

The Lights dim. All action freezes

Narrator (*off*) There they are upon a German hill-top on a summer's day in nineteen thirty-eight. Thunder clouds roll over them. They have their separate and shared hopes and ambitions and fears. But they are young and are confident that even their troubles will be surmountable. However, we who watch them from the uplands of a future time know things they do not know, cannot even guess at. Fiona will have her abortion. Frank, somehow, will come up trumps with the money, and the man in Harley Street will come up trumps with his skill and discretion. Then a little time later, Fiona and Frank will gradually drift apart, not so much falling out of love, as directing themselves on to diverging paths in their quests for personal fulfilment. Three years from now Frank, a fighter pilot, will die defending western civilization: another life aborted, so to speak, under the cruel compulsions of the age. Fiona, hearing of this tragedy, will briefly mourn, but her job in the Admiralty will be demanding and she will give herself to it with the kind of desperate enthusiasm into which ambition, at moments of crisis, often transforms itself. Eventually she will make a wartime marriage to a naval commander from the United States, and after the war she will go to New York. Some years of marriage will follow, and then divorce. But she will stay on in New York, a bright, astute executive in a bold, brash, advertising agency. Another marriage, another divorce, a lot of affairs, and a seat upon the board of the corporation she serves so well. She is in New York now, still working, still a driving force, an example and inspiration to those who follow in her footsteps. Childless, she lives alone in a luxury penthouse far above the city, and in her limited spare time, by way of relaxation, takes karate lessons, so as to be prepared to defend herself against the inevitable mugger, the unavoidable rapist. Poppy will get her inheritance from Great-Aunt Ethel—only a half share, the other half going to a home for stray cats. Anyway, Ethel will take such an unconscionable time a-dying that her estate will be sadly depleted before Poppy and the cats get hands and claws on it. Poppy in wartime will do her bit rehabilitating evacuees and refugees and homeless victims of the blitz. She will do her work conscientiously, but with no deep involvement. Come the peace, she will marry a country-town lawyer, have two sons and two daughters, and will grow fat, because of an excessive intake of carbohydrates, and grow prematurely old, because she finds old age to be the most placid, comfortable time of her life. Dennis will, much to his own surprise, be an intelligence officer during the war, and, after that, will find himself sucked into the Foreign Office. He will marry a very well-bred girl with no sense of humour and together they will beget a very well-bred family. Dennis will devote himself to the pursuit of moderation in all things and, for the most part, will succeed. In his late middle-age he will encounter a young man who very much reminds him of Frank Chaseforth and he will come dangerously close to embarking upon an illicit sexual relationship. At the last moment, however, he will reject the young man, accepting, instead, the offer of the knighthood that has been long desired by his wife. He will sleep the rest of his life away in the comfort of a leather armchair in his gentleman's club, occasionally dreaming of times past, absent friends, times that never were, and loves abandoned. Karl will freeze to death somewhere in Russia in nineteen forty-two. Only at the very last will his poor, snow-numbed mind admit that no Austrian house-painter should ever have been given the right to demand such a sacrifice from him.

Karl's tears of regret for wasted years will freeze upon his dead cheeks. And Esther . . .

Esther enters R. *She is now dressed in the pyjama-striped dress of the concentration camp inmate. She moves downstage and stands there, facing the audience*

No, even from our vantage point in time, we cannot pretend to know exactly Esther's fate, because, for all our knowledge, despite our professed empathy and sympathy, we are incapable of imagining what life will really be like for Esther after this day upon the hill-top. Civilized minds, such as ours, cannot even begin to grasp at the landscape of horror and desolation that will be Esther's future. Esther must be for us, as she was for those others on the hill, a spectre who haunts us—sometimes on the cinema and television screens, or in the pages of books we barely care to read—as a warning against both ourselves and others. She is a wraith who reminds us, when we have the courage to let her, that the impossible, the unimaginable, does happen. For that reason, the spirit of Esther will live alongside those other five lives, and, if there is to be hope for a time to come, her spirit must outlive us all

Karl comes to attention, gives the Nazi salute, turns and exits R

Frank Let's get out of this beastly place before the downpour.
Fiona (*putting her arm around Frank's waist*) Don't feel too badly. You know you tried your best. No-one can do more than that.
Dennis Hey, Poppy, I'll carry the gramophone.
Poppy Not bloody likely. (*Pauses*) But, if you like, you may take my hand to help me make the descent.
Dennis My pleasure. It'll probably be a lot easier going downhill.

With Frank and Fiona going first, arms linked around each other, and Dennis and Poppy, hand in hand, going after, all four exit R

Esther, unmoving, remains after the others have left the stage

Pause

Faintly is heard the sound of many voices, murmuring and wailing

Voices (*off*) Move! Move! Move!

Sound of dogs barking savagely and of running footsteps upon cobble-stones

Voices (*off, shouting harshly*) On to the trucks! Come along, get on
  to those trucks! Move! Move! Move!

*A woman screams, children sob. Then is heard the revving up of
many motors, followed by the sound of trucks being driven away.
The sound of the trucks grows loud and then slowly dwindles away*

Silent pause

Thunder crashes loudly

Lights fade to Black-out

CURTAIN

FURNITURE AND PROPERTY LIST

On stage: Bare except for backcloth of blue sky above a place of greenery

Off stage: Picnic basket containing chequered cloth, cutlery, crockery, glasses etc. **(Frank)**
Portable gramophone **(Poppy)**

Personal: **Frank:** silk cravat
Dennis: Tyrolean hat
Karl: Sam Browne type belt with a leather-holstered revolver

LIGHTING PLOT

Property fittings required: nil

Exterior. The same scene throughout

To open:	Full general lighting	
Cue 1	Sound of more thunder	(Page 21)
	Lights dim	
Cue 2	**Karl** exits	(Page 23)
	Increase lighting	
Cue 3	Thunder crashes loudly	(Page 24)
	Fade to Black-out	

EFFECTS PLOT

MADE AND PRINTED IN GREAT BRITAIN BY
LATIMER TREND & COMPANY LTD, PLYMOUTH
MADE IN ENGLAND